Seren of the Wildwood

Marly Youmans

Copyright © 2023 Wiseblood Books

All rights reserved, including the right to reproduce this book or any portions thereof in any form whatsoever except for brief quotations in book reviews. For information, address the publisher:

> Wiseblood Books
> P.O. Box 870
> Menomonee Falls, WI 53052

Printed in the United States of America

Set in Baskerville URW Typesetting

Cover Design & Interior Illustrations: Clive Hicks-Jenkins

ISBN 13: Paperback: 978-1-951319-64-9

Hardcover: 978-1-951319-65-6

Wiseblood Books

To Mat. Maureen and Fr. James Krueger
of Cloud-Bearing Mountain

There were giants in the earth . . .

Genesis 6:4

. . . in faërian drama you are in a dream
that some other mind is weaving . . .

Tolkien, *On Fairy-Stories*

Two-thirds of him is god, one-third of him is human.

The Epic of Gilgamesh, tr. Kovacs

Seren of the Wildwood

Prolegomenon, in the voice of Wren

The wildwood holds the remnants of the past,
Strange ceremonies that the fays still love
To watch—the rituals of demon tribes
Who once played havoc with the universe,
And everything that says the world is not
Exactly what it seems is hidden here,
But also there are paths to blessedness.
An elvish skill disguises cruelty,
And well we know that fairies can be so,
Spying out the weaknesses of humans,
Spilling over with a manic laughter
Portending something fearsome yet to come…
In finer times they strew the land with blooms
And ramble, singing in the wildwood's heart.
In long ago, in times crumbled to dust,
The fallen angels once explored the lands
And mated with the women of the world;
Though few remain, they stream invisible
Through every cranny of the wildwood realm,
And when they may, they catch the innocent
To hoodwink girls or torment heedless boys.
    Enough!
   I've said too many things;
   The wildwood is a tough
   Terrain, yet beauty springs
   Like diamonds from the rough.

1.

Never speak your passions by the wildwood—
The heedfulness that might have saved their lives
From harm was torn in two, and afterward
They were dismayed, bewildered by surprise.
The father looked as handsome as a dream
Of elvishness, a man whose element
Seemed fire, his aura crackling energy,
His potent green-eyed glance a stream of sparks;
The mother softer, secretive, blue-eyed,
Her element not fire but water: force
That mines the roots of mountains, flies to clouds…
Was he too proud a flame, too rich in youth?
Did she demand too much in quietness?
Or did their beauty lure the wildwood's stare?
Of course, he was the one to speak the words,
Sudden, wrathful, turning on the children,
Two little boys who leaped in reckless joy
And never thought of punishment and doom.
"I wish I had a daughter, not you boys
Who shut your ears and are no help to me!"
The edge of things is always dangerous,
         And trees
    May shelter eyes and ears
    That do not care to please—
    The shade where something hears,
    The dark where something sees.

2.

What hears and laughs at us from wildwood leaves?
Is it the fays, the faded ones who slip
And weave through leaves and branches soundlessly,
The tall medieval elves who sing of loss?
Is it mere fairies, dwindled down from elves,
Or else made small and soulless from the start?
Might it be demons, curled in flower cups
And murmuring a malediction song—
Or do the fallen angels seek out shade,
Their spirits winding to and fro like snakes,
Each seeking to seduce some human soul
In darkness underneath the wildwood's boughs?
Whatever breeze it was that stirred the leaves,
Some rustling presence marked the father's cry
And laughed to hear the spill of thoughtless words,
So that he paused and turned uneasily
To face the trees before he shepherded
His sons toward home—but from that very day,
They changed, diminishing from what had been,
Their merriment at ebb, their features thin,
Their eyes the wisdom-wells of suffering…
              What power
        Led him that very night
        To seed the woman's flower?
        Who called a child toward light
        From her conception's hour?

3.

And so the little boys went sickening
Into the darkness, mystery, and fate,
Though no one knew a good wherefore, or why
The infant in her mother's belly thrived
As if she drank her brothers' strength away.
They four—the mother, brothers, unborn babe—
Lay slumbering or waking on the bed,
The two dwindling, one grieving, one swelling.
The father boiled spring water in a shell
And called upon the air to bring sons home,
To banish changelings from their hearth: no use,
No earthly use, for that was not their doom.
The mother labored hard and bore a girl
As brimming-full of health as a fresh plum,
So that they marveled at her coloring
And beauty, though the mother also wept,
For weariness and sadness ruled her days.
That night the parents dreamed the selfsame dream
Of healing, fragrant flames on the hearthstone
And brothers playing, laughing in the fire…
Who turned to smile and give one radiant look.
          Morning
       Brought long-expected news,
       Cauled mirror, sounds of mourning,
       A sunrise like a bruise,
       Woe despite forewarning.

4.

Fresh woven in the mornings for three days,
The wreaths of violets and forget-me-nots
Cradled the heads of boys who seemed to sleep
Within a fragrant box of applewood,
While in the yard, the wings from fresh-planed trim
Were stirred and lifted by an idle breeze,
As if such thoughtless things could wish to fly.
The rosy child was passed from hand to hand,
Neighbors finding solace in the new;
The father hunched alone, his bandaged hands
Held awkwardly before the scrap-fed fire;
The mother couldn't be made comforted
But paced and cried along the forest's edge,
Her hair disheveled and her clothing torn.
And when the time was come to tuck the boys
To sleep like dormant seeds inside the ground,
She struck the boards as if to smash a way
Into the night of earth that held such stars…
Later, the father and the mother lay
Not touching, no, nor lightening their pain,
Marooned upon the ice flow of the sheets.
    The ark
  Of cradle rocked the child
  Who babbled to a spark
  Of star—by light beguiled
  In the unbrothered dark.

5.

A strange beginning for a human babe,
To watch her mother's face be like a sky
With skimming clouds and flashes of bright beams
But also rain in downpours without end
Or sleet and snow that comes down soft and deep
And wants to cover everything in white
Until the world is still with sleep and hush.
One day the mother kneeled to hook a chain
Around the baby's throat, with heart of lead
To warm against the skin and make her tug
The heavy, unaccustomed thing away…
And stamped on the soft metal were two words,
MY SAVIOR, for the mother said the child
Had saved her from the madness of raw grief.
And once the girl went toddling out-of-doors
So that her mother shrieked and fled to look
In well and cellar and the verge of woods,
As wild with fear as she had been before,
Until she found her sitting in an isle
Of summer buds and flowers washed by sun
And tended by the buzz of honeybees,
As if she had been drawn by loveliness
             Or some
        Siren hum in nature
        That lured the child to come,
        To see, to adventure:
        Creation's secret thrum.

6.

She spired up in a solitude of three
Remembering the two who'd gone before,
Her father sometimes bursting forth with fire
Or hardening to silences of ice
She was too young to brook and comprehend
Or even ask what such harsh weathers meant
That flamed or froze her childhood to the bone.
And once she dreamed her mother cinched a leash,
Invisible but strong, around her wrist
So she could never ramble far away
And lose herself in cloudy distances—
As if the mother could have kept her sons
From wandering in regions ruled by death
By strings and strength of mind and spirit's force.
The wildwood sang her name as evening fell
And made her wakeful, restless in her bed,
Unsure if what she heard might only be
The breezes soughing in the canopy,
Sighing *Seren, Seren, Seren, Seren*
While she, bedazzled, stared past windowpanes
At the angelic bonfires of the stars.
    The snow
   Of starlight filled her dreams
   With an enchanted glow,
   Its otherworldly gleams
   Dislodging gloom and woe.

7.

How singular it was to see her dance
Around the brothers' grave, to hear her sing
Of thoughts and longings to an eerie tune,
As if they listened from the ground and knew
Her joys or sorrows and could sympathize
With how she plucked a music from the air
And added childish words and images.
Her veneration of the brothers found
Its form this way, as in the candles lit
And fists of flowers gathered, left to wilt
And fade away beneath the sun or moon—
Tokens that said when precious things are lost,
They leave an absence that's made evident
And takes a shape in sorrow and in songs.
When breezes crept out from the canopy
To rustle skirts and nudge the drying blooms,
Then Seren seemed to wake to mysteries
Hiding near the margins of the wildwood
And dashed along the forest's crooked edge,
Daring the hidden beings in the trees
To come into the sun and show themselves.
    One day
   Spoke secrets to the next…
   And night-time's starry play
   Wheeled calmly on, unvexed
   By dreams of mortal clay.

8.

At fifteen, Seren climbed a mountain ash
To better hear the wildwood's murmurings
That lured her on, said she was beautiful,
In mind unlike the other, lesser girls—
She listened long in wonder, shivering,
Until her name came clanging on the air,
Its syllables a spell to bring her home.
Her mother meant that she should learn to be
Alone, without a man or children's claim,
That she should do some high and lonely thing,
Like a secret princess in a tower
With no demands on her except the ones
That come with birth and are impossible
To flee, for they are written in the blood.
But Seren more and more was drawn to walk
The border where the sun gave way to shade
And ancient darkness found a way to speak
In moving leaves or airs that kissed a cheek,
Although at night it seemed to her the stars
Were not angelic friends as once they seemed,
But burned with warning, set against the night,
         Opposed
    To duskiness and cloud
    And what it was that dozed
    Or woke to speak in boughed
    Shadow—concealed, enclosed.

9.

To Seren, all the world seemed liminal,
Its solid self desiring to be mist,
To fall away and form into the new,
A land with shapes and colors never seen,
Where neither fire nor cold could mar a child,
Where death was seized and tied up with a bow,
Where brothers might walk barefoot on the grass.
So she began to climb the nearest trees,
Hoisting herself into the canopy
To see the dragonflies and bees alight
On leaves of hornbeam, yellowwood, or oak,
And peek into a wilderness of green,
But most of all to hear the verdant notes
And whispers that inhabited the woods.
With just a few short steps into the shade,
She found the voices of her parents died,
And only the lead heart around her neck
Reminded her of duty, or that she
Was named the infant savior who must live
And never dare to go adventuring
In realms inhabited by mysteries.
            What glides
      And glimmers in the trees,
      What half is shown, half hides,
      What murmurs on the breeze:
      These were her wildwood guides.

10.

Because she listened to the wildwood's song,
She turned away from home and those who loved
Her shape and voice and her unstudied grace,
And though they were imperfect humankind,
This mother, father, and the presences
Of ghostly brothers standing in between,
They each had cared for Seren in their way.
At first she tied a sort of maypole thread
Around a bole and wandered into shade,
And napped on leaves and let the branch-combed wind
Lift the strands of hair and press against her,
As if it might be some invisible
Eros, lover from the Psyche story,
And she the princess to be sacrificed.
But soon she learned to scale the highest trees
And gaze across the tapestry of greens
Resembling what she thought must be the sea
That tossed with turbulence or gently waved,
And all the while a voice was whispering
Its flattery, its stories of desire
In far-off kingdoms where she might be queen.
              At home,
      She sleep-walked through the day,
      Her trance of gauze and gloom
      A faërian stage play,
      A dream where she could roam.

11.

One morning in the trees she met a girl
Who seemed but scarcely older than herself,
Though frail and wan and shivering with cold,
Who drifted through the forest like a wraith,
And Seren wondered at her delicate
Twig-like limbs, the clouds of floating hair,
And green-eyed glance that found no place to rest.
"No, no, said Lia, "no, I cannot go
With you or stay, not anywhere near woods,
But force myself to travel till I reach
A leafless place of sun beside the sea,
Where are no voices wildering the air
With promises and spite, and no occult
Beings one-third man and two-thirds daemon.
"You're young as yet," she said, "and there are things
In Wildwood that will slay the heart of you—
That slew the child, the innocent in me,
So do not roam the deepest woods or seek
For answers to the runic mysteries
But linger, happy by the hearth of home,
Content to be unknowing and unknown."
  And here
She gazed about, alarmed,
And breathed, "Conserve your fear
To shield you from what harmed
My soul, should he appear."

12.

Then Lia fled and vanished into light
That like a portal sparked between two trees,
Leaving Seren to ponder what she meant,
Forgetting for a time to heed the words
That wove and fluttered through the canopy
As if they might be little feathered snakes
That flocked and flew, maneuvering to sky.
But long-tried custom says a prophet is
To be ignored, and Seren was no more
Than any mortal, apt to make mistakes
And prone to think herself the chosen one,
To sense the verge of something wonderful
Just up ahead, tomorrow or the next
To bring a green sunrise and mighty quest.
She might have stayed near home a week or more,
Weaving wreaths for long-lost brothers' grave mounds
And wishing they would resurrect from earth
Like figures trooping out of fairy hills,
Until one afternoon she swept the floor,
Did the dishes, combed her mother's long hair,
And, tempted, ventured into wildwood shade.
          The words
     Of Lia's warnings were
     Forgotten omen-birds
     That whirred away from her:
     On such a lapse fate turns.

13.

She dared go deep into the forest's heart,
Singing a ballad made of love and doom,
And as she went, another voice joined hers,
Its low, seductive music spiraling
Around the tale some village bard once dreamed
And sung to old and young beside a fire,
For joys and tragedies are always news.
Because she knew no word or name for him,
She called him Ariel—invisible,
Mysterious, long heard in rustling leaves,
By now familiar in his flattery;
She wondered if he could be fairy, sprite,
Angelic virtue, cherubim, or throne,
Or simply a chimera of her mind.
That day he murmured passionate desires
That fell like royal drops of indigo
To stain with dye day-dreaming reveries
And make her wish for an incarnate boy
To clasp her hand and saunter through the trees,
And in some glade to pause and kiss her lips
Under sun and wink of a crescent moon.
    A thrill
  Of yearning flowered deep
  In Seren, flashed its chill
  Through her, and roused from sleep
  A woman's ardent will.

14.

Then Ariel began to lure her far
From home and father, mother, little graves—
From all who ever cared to know she lived,
And so she wandered out of lands she knew
And into unfamiliar, darker paths
Where light came spindling down through thickset leaves
That shuddered at the wind's caressing stroke.
When ferns and boughs became her makeshift bed
And rest dispelled the ramblings of the day,
A presence slipped into her dreams and turned
Her sleep to jumbles of nightmarish scenes
That made her wake in fright and cry for home
Till Ariel with crooning lullabies
Chased away the fearsome images.
But buoyant morning makes the world anew;
She washed herself and finger-raked her hair,
Content a while to walk in wilderness
With no more friend than unseen Ariel,
Master of milk-and-honey blandishments
Who fed delusion with his promises
And raised up golden castles in the air:
>   He wrought
> Nothing sad or tragic—
> A paradise of thought,
> Sweet illusion's magic,
> Some flawless Camelot.

15.

All morning Ariel was murmuring
Some story meant to pleasantly beguile:
A Queen sat sewing by a window-frame,
The windowsill as black as ebony,
Wood starred with snow and royal drops of blood...
She dreamed a child of red and black and white,
Although that life would be the death of hers.
Mid-tale, they came upon a riddling sight,
A tree that Seren thought was dead or else
An artificial, sculpted tower-shape
That, smooth and leafless, spired toward heaven's gate,
With one side jet, the other silver-white—
Like magicked apples in a fairy tale
With one fair cheek, the other poisonous.
With subtlety and stealth, now Ariel
Began to urge that Seren climb toward sky
And master this conundrum of a tree,
Explore enigma, ban bewilderment,
And he would wind around her limbs and waist
To steady her along the Babel way
Until they brushed the ceiling's clouds and blue:
         She laughed
     To think that they could catch
     That airy hue—how daft,
     When anyone who'd snatch
     The sky would need witchcraft.

16.

Yet up she climbed, the black and silver-white
Resistant to her touch, as hard as stone
And not at all resembling living bark,
The tree—if tree it was—an anti-tree,
The curving blades of branches sharp to hands,
Unfriendly to the little animals
And birds that love to nest in canopies.
The voice of Ariel was lost in sounds
Of Seren's breath, the beating of her heart,
Ears ringing like a frenzied carillon,
While blossoming inside her as she climbed
Was fright that lit her veins and sped her pulse,
Her mesh of nerves a black and silver tree
That caged the flickerings of butterflies.
From pinnacles above the other trees,
She saw the green infinitude of leaves
And shuddered, cowering against the bole,
The sun outlandish to her darkened eyes,
Its sudden fires transfiguring the world;
Sight dazzled by its rays, she clenched her lids
And covered up her ears against the sound
        Of a bell:
    She swayed, lacking a clasp
    On forking jet, and fell
    Down with a headlong gasp
    And terror-stricken yell.

17.

She slept and woke and slept again, and found
On next awaking that she sprawled on stone
Before a pyre and idol cast from lead;
The surface danced with bonfire jollity,
Behemoth bulk up-loomed, and parted lips
Breathed a sigh and murmuringly spoke
In tones that had the mark of Ariel.
"Don't be afraid; exult, for you have won
The blazing love you fancied in your dreams,
And you will be the mother of a child,
A son whose titan genealogy
Is only one-third bound to humankind,
And one-third godly mine, and one-third owed
To a god-and-mortal instrument, the king."
Although her heart was running in full flight,
Seren glimpsed no path for an escape,
For unfamiliar limestone walls reared high,
And all was barren save a bed of gold,
The fire, and statue made of lead and breath…
But from the cold, flung shadow of the god,
She whispered a refusal to his pledge.
          Yet what
     Good are words of a girl
     Against a coil of plot,
     Against an Ariel,
     Against a braided knot?

18.

The dark, three-stranded plot of Ariel
Plaited as one a girl, god-king, and god—
Or if not god, a once-angelic thing,
One of those who slid from sky like stars
So long ago that men just can't believe
They ever were, and women fail to hide
The glory of their hair from spirit eyes.
The shouts of people at the iron doors
Meant their hero-king was near, one worshipped
As a ruling god yet also bending
In adoration to the leaden bulk
Of idol-Ariel, though stupefied
By fumes, by drink infused with seeds and spells
That bring on dreams in rites of sacrifice.
If Seren dreamed of Eros, what she met
Was never Eros, slim and elegant:
First priestesses who pressed their wine on her
Till Seren reeled and lost all syllables
Save as something slithering, suspiring
The idol emanated. Next, a king
Not young but middle-aged, his curling beard
    Gone steel,
  His mind turned lunatic,
  His body no ideal
  Of grace and charm to prick
  Desire: man as ordeal.

19.

The Seren who had fed on fairy tales
And legends of stout-hearted, noble knights
Was unprepared for Ariel's designs,
Or for a lover who demolished dreams
(A monolith colliding with the soil
To crush the innocence that happened near)
And slammed into her body like a sword.
The mating lasted minutes and was spent,
And she was loam turned over by the plow,
The vessel for the metaphysical
Semen of Ariel and kingly sperm,
And afterward there was a royal shrug
And exit, while the idol slept and snored
As men do after sex or lavish meals.
What else could Seren do but weep for hurt,
For high indifference and lack of love,
And drag herself away, to scrub her skin
In river-water turbulent with foam
And falls, and then to cross its pounding width,
To set some barrier between herself
And the story of a demonic day,
    To tell
  Herself that loss would end,
  That love can break a spell,
  That days to come might mend
  The ravages of hell.

20.

Seren thought more kindly of her father
And mother as she traveled through the trees,
Remembering the days that showed a care
For her and what she might mature to be,
And how they often talked beside the fire,
Laughing and telling stories of the past
And how they'd come to live beside the woods.
She missed her room, the wardrobe with her things:
The gown, already spattered with her blood,
Was snagged on prickly thorns of eglantine,
While hawthorn spines assailed the tender silk,
And all the world seemed thistle, bramble, barb,
Without a hideaway where she might rest
And gather strength and wisdom for return.
At night, she slept on moss and drifts of leaves
And woke to feel the beads of morning dew
That settled on her face, and scoured the brush
For berries, or else dug familiar roots—
And sometimes, tentative, she tried to eat
Some nameless plant that, sampled once, she shunned
Forever after, never bit again,
        A bane
    To any human life:
    Calamity of pain,
    A buried, twisting knife,
    Ruination's reign.

21.

"Don't be afraid," a figure called to her
When once she stumbled on another soul,
A fellow nomad in the wilderness.
"Then what's your name?" she asked, "for I've learned this:
Never to make up names for strangers here,
But to compass who they are before I
Am willing to put faith in friendly words."
"You might well call me Aidan, as some do—
I have too many names, but that one's good,
As golden as December's pleasant flames
When your father rouses sunrise-early
And feeds a resinous bonfire with pine
So that your mother may be pleased with glow
And warmth despite the bitter wintertide."
"My father and my mother? Do you know
Our house that's poised between the woods and fields,
Beside my brothers' graves, and how some swear
Uncanny sprites go roving on the edge
And sometimes hear us talk, and laugh and cast
Some wicked spell to bring catastrophe—
And might you be some creature of that sort,
         Who tends
    Toward rascal roguery
    And devilment that ends
    Fearsomely in worry
    And loss that never mends?"

22.

And Aidan paused, debating what to say:
"Through workings of a temple ritual,
An act of darkness that makes angels quail,
You are with child—forbidden child who is
One-third mortal and two-thirds god, the spawn
Of an anointed king and Ariel,
Though that, indeed, is not his proper name."
"What madness! Sheerest nonsense," Seren said,
Not believing, yet in seconds half-sure;
"And what are you, revealing hidden news
That comes to even me as a surprise,
Unwelcome and unwished-for? To recall
Details and contemplate the origin
Of such a baby shocks my memory."
"Merely a messenger who brings the word,
Or call me friend to wildwood wanderers
Stumbling on the realm of fallen beings
And kings long worshipped as divinities—
That is, to you, the traipser in the trees
So far from home, in need of anchorage
And help and haven from the elements.
               For this
      I came: to counsel, guide,
      Make sure you do not miss
      A port where you may bide,
      And find some fleeting bliss.

23.

"In times to come, you may be glad again,
Though not for some great while, and then you may
Turn over fading leaves of memory,
Considering and wondering at lost
Days past, and out from mulch of time a tree
May sprout and aim to sky, a glistening
Verdant tower of rejoicing, Seren....
If you'll accept a crumb of help from me,
Trek westward till you find a riverbank
And cross by means of rocks that travelers
Have heaved to aid their fellows on the way,
A sinuous but broken line to bridge
The waters' tantrum under cataracts
That fractures, flashes, cleaves the bed of stone."
"I don't know what you're saying," Seren cried,
But Aidan only climbed into a tree,
Calling down that she should find the woman
That seekers termed Greenmother; soon he passed
From Seren's gaze, his progress lost in leaves,
Hid by sun, though whether clambered skyward
Or swinging lightly branch to branch was murk
   And mist
  To Seren's watching eyes:
  And their mid-forest tryst
  Might clasp the truth or lies
  Or both in braided twist.

24.

That day she happened on a shallow course
Of water running sibilant and quick
On stones long polished by the nudge of waves,
A road of agates, infinite as stars,
And beautiful to touch and contemplate,
The colors bright, submerged beneath a skin
Like glass, a river like a crystal snake.
Delighted by the hues and clarity,
She stripped away her clothes and cautiously
Lowered herself into streaming waters
Until she lay against the riverbed,
Its jeweled chroma pressed against her flesh,
Her bones invigorated by the cold,
Her mass of hair a glory on the flow.
She added tears to the tributary flood,
Though hardly understanding why she wept,
And whether it was for world's loveliness
Or for her parents and the little graves,
Or treachery, betrayal, bitterness;
Perhaps it was for all of these at once,
The intricate entanglement of life,
    The way
  A single tale's a plait
  Of many threads, the way
  Hued agates may create
  A rainbow, road, bouquet....

25.

Floating, bobbing on the surface, Seren
Pressed one hand against her belly: nothing
Was unfamiliar but a cloying scent,
As if a child—if child it was—might mean
Fragrant transformation, transmutation
To something she had never known or wished,
The simple mystery of motherhood.
After the gown she scrubbed with soapwort leaves
Hung drying in the branches of a tree,
Seren finger-combed her raveled tangles,
Sitting naked on a sun-baked boulder,
And wove some sandals from the river cane,
Lacing them with cords of braided fiber
To shield her feet from spurs of grit and thorn.
And next she found a walking stick and set
Her feet to trudging forward once again,
For though she loved the rainbowed agate stones
And crystal water, this was not the stream
That Aidan promised, where a flash of sun
Ignited mist with spears of slantwise light
And thunder broke from rocks and waterfalls.
    "Fey land,"
  She said, "of filigree
  And force and dazzling sand:
  Look kindly on me: be
  Less fierce, less wild, less grand."

26.

Now Seren judged the past more tenderly,
Saw how misfortune warped her family,
Thrusting apart a husband and a wife
Until each stood upon a precipice
And stared across a spreading canyon rift,
One hopeless and one angry, both alone
Though always in the other's line of sight.
In this way, Seren came to pity them,
Man and woman flensed of gentleness,
Unable to restore their peace once more,
Unsatisfied with how the other mourned,
One seemingly gone desolation-mad,
The other whipping fires of anguish deep
Into the secret places of the soul.
The land around grew tilted, hillier;
Astonished at how far she'd come from home,
Seren climbed up high enough to wonder
At water-dragon coils and serpent-streams,
And in the distance heard impetuous
Music of many waters thundering
Against the boulders of a riverbed.
          Spellbound
     And snared by loveliness,
     She listened, looked, and found
     A longing self's not less
     But more when lost in sound.

27.

Land slanted further, treacherous with chert
That tore the basketry of Seren's shoes,
Making her pause to fiddle with the weave
Time and again, until she reached a hut
And stopped to soak a while in forenoon sun,
Sandal-tinkering with twining grasses
And relishing the warmth against her skin.
Mid-day, an ancient man emerged from trees
Above the stony cot and called to her:
His name was Cavan, and for many years
He'd been the master of this minor perch
In wilderness, and ruled the birds and squirrels
And all that crept or slithered in the weeds;
He bore an angler's pole and string of fish.
"I must've known good company might come,
To cast so well above the waterfall,"
He said; and gutting little shining trout,
He speared them on a stick to roast in fire:
"I never tasted anything so fine
At home," she said, "or in my wanderings,
Away from comforts found in cottages."
           Seren
               Perceived death's bald details
               On rock: bright eye, fair fin;
               Observed fine starry scales
               On stones, bleak and barren.

28.

For seven days and nights she stayed to rest,
Roosting in a hammock strung from tree trunks,
Hanging, rocking with the turning world
Between the earth and sky, and dreaming dreams
She marveled at, on waking with the dawn;
All day she listened, learned from Cavan's talk
The way to find the falls and upward paths.
The old man wore a threadbare purple robe
That looked to be regalia from a past
More rich and lavish in its mode than this,
Although he never spoke of years before
But told of trees that joined the sky to earth
And stars that sang of mysteries to men,
Or of the secrets hid in fairy tales.
And when he spoke and gestured with his hands,
The wrens and finches swooped to him to peck
The crumbs from lap and ground, and songbirds trilled
Their messages of sky from nearby trees,
And once or twice they plucked a curling thread
Of Cavan's beard and flew to weave a nest
In coverts or high places in the woods.
          Wisdom
    Balanced lightly on him;
    Like sunshine's freight, his sum
    Of thought could make air brim
    With lively fizz and thrum.

29.

She woke and caught him dancing by the fire
At midnight, robe sashaying to and fro
And beard ascending, falling with the tune
As Cavan crooned a song of agéd men
Who totter in the breeze and tumble in
Small star-reflecting ponds when drunk on wine,
Reciting poetry to please the moon.
But in the morning, all was as before,
The elder plunking down his bowls of seeds
And nuts and sun-dried berries for a meal,
So Seren wondered if the dance she saw
Was real or just a fancy from a dream,
Though didn't ask, sensing the weather's change,
Unexpected air of melancholy.
"I'll be musing of you often, Seren,"
He said; "an ancient likes to see the young
Come trooping by and pause to perch a while,
But you'll be leaving now to brave the falls
On crossing-stones contrived by wayfarers
And reach Greenmother's sheltered garden house,
For she can be some benefit to you."
   Regret
  And gladness blend as one
  At times—who can forget,
  When fairy tales are done,
  Their magic alphabet?

30.

When Seren left, she bore away a sack
Of grain and seeds, and from her shoulders hung
A cape of rabbit fur, the workmanship
Of Cavan in his younger, spryer days,
A help for morning warmth or evening sleep,
And more than these she felt his farewell words
That wished for Seren strength in motherhood.
And so she traveled toward the roar of rain
With thunder, apprehensive as she neared
The lip where torrents catapulted free
From stone and merged into a muscular
And sovereign streaming force—the energy
That shocks the trembling pebbles into flight
And grinds the massive boulders into bowls.
The brunt, the force of falls made Seren gasp
When she reached the pool and met the headlong
Drop of waters, and glimpsed a cliff-wall cave
Behind the veils, and on projecting rock
A figure standing naked in the flood
Who answered Seren's call to learn her name:
"I am the Oracle of Cataracts,
        And you
    May ask me what you will,
    And I will tell you true—
    Like water, I can spill
    And make the world anew.

31.

"For flood has often changed the shape of things,
Obliterating towns and families,
Judging the times to be in need of rinse
And transformation—just the way my words
Can alter watercourses of the mind
And stir the thoughts of many when I spill—
We oracles speak little but say much."
To Seren, it seemed marvelous that she
Could hear the oracle above the pour,
And surely she would benefit from help…
But still she hesitated, did not ask
Because she thought of Ariel and how
So many falls find genesis in talk,
A cordial chat, a civil tête-à-tête.
Cavan had not aimed to alter Seren
But told her tales, or how to win the falls
And the woman whom he called Greenmother—
This oracle, so pale and sinuous,
Arms undulating in ascending mist,
Was no Greenmother, and perhaps was more
Like Ariel, whose words proved sinister.
   Although
  She ached to know what must
  Be found and where to go,
  She couldn't lose mistrust's
  Cloudiness and shadow.

32.

And yet, despite the cautionary fear
That sprang from what she knew of Ariel
—Betrayer, adversary, ruin's friend—
She asked a question of the oracle,
Almost as if she asked it of herself,
Slowly murmuring to the cataract,
"What don't I see, what don't I recognize?"
The laughter of the oracle rang out:
"Your household lares and penates shake,
Their stubby naked feet tremble in boots,
Their little woven hats wobble on heads,
Their chubby gold or stone or silver limbs
Are tremulous with fear of what shall be,
Are tremulous with fear of *who* shall be.
The fright in drops on gold or silver skin
Is beading, swelling, trickling down an arm,
The sweat on steatite is gathering,
And sudor red with blood pools in the eyes
That stare to see abomination's birth:
But you see nothing, neither minor gods
Nor what it is that's seeded in your womb."
        Naive,
           Already once beguiled,
           Her heart prone to believe,
           Seren the woman-child
           Was easy to deceive.

33.

And yet her ignorance was paradise,
For talk of lares and penates was
Greek to Seren, and all the oracle
Could say was wash and waterfall to her;
Then she remembered Cavan's courtesy
And kindness, how he told her where to bridge
The pool by rocks arranged by travelers.
She searched the water's brink and found a ledge
That seemed to point into the roil of cloud,
And next to it a boulder, scored and gouged,
That could be something like a starting point,
A span to cross from here to there, though mist
Obscured the way, and water made it slick
And treacherous to leap from stone to stone.
Cavan's tales of princesses and peasants
Who ranged east of the sun and west of moon
And met a realm unknown to mapmakers
Inspired her bravery to pierce the brume,
To dare the splash and seethe below the chute,
To trust that unknown steppingstones to come
Would be revealed in mysteries of cloud.
           Jilted
    Words of the oracle
    Were unavailing milt,
    Phantasmagorical
    Flowers—seedless, wilted.

34.

Inside the clouds, the water roared its news
Of power's tabernacle, feral-free,
And Seren shouted back in wild surprise,
In love with froth and thrust and energies
Invading her with poured vitality,
Surrounding her—a moving, breathing room,
A fairy region where she moved and breathed.
A sudden brightening of summer sun
Transformed the vapor to a brilliant white,
Its dazzle struck through by prismatic spokes,
A misty rainbow glow—and Seren stopped
In pleasure, though a momentary wave
Of nausea made her stoop to kneel on stones
As if the child in her disliked the light.
Cloud wrapped her in embrace as she advanced
From stone to stone, navigating the gaps
And sliding on the pebbles heaped in mounds,
The gift of those who passed that way before…
And when she skipped from the last rock to shore,
The soaked green grass seemed many elfin flags
That stood upright and spoke of beauty's reign.
    Their cheer
   Was simple and direct,
   A thing forthright and clear,
   Each blade new-washed and flecked,
   Each drop a crystal tear.

35.

Her time inside the cloud was like a song
Of danger mixed with joyful jubilee,
And like a dream it fled away and seemed
To be a brighter version of her life
Like some intrusion from another world
Where color and intensity were charged
And changed in nature from what was before.
She felt a victory, for she had crossed
The thunderous pool, escaped the drowning place,
And surely she had met and passed a test,
A step upon the way to something else,
Although she didn't know its whereabouts,
And what might be the pitfalls of the path
Or gradient along the mountain's slope.
Gazing up the rock face toward the cave,
She saw the Oracle of Cataracts
Mouth some message, meaning lost in deluge,
And caught her breath because the shape was such
A wraith, phantasm, apparition—death's
Impression drawn as pallid lamia,
A demon horror of decaying flesh,
        As if
    Her hour for prophecies
    And life inside the cliff
    Was past—a faded frieze,
    A scratched-out petroglyph.

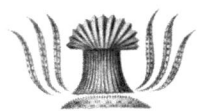

36.

Having no truck with tales of household gods,
She shivered but dismissed the prophecies
The Oracle of Cataracts proclaimed,
Setting her face toward the mountaintops
That rose ahead in far blue distances,
Determined to discover what there was
In heights above the fields and woods she knew.
She climbed a hillside slashed by terraces
Where plants she'd never seen were blossoming
And fruiting on supports and trellises,
Though nowhere did she see a gardener
Or anyone with basket and a knife,
Out cutting greens or picking broccoli
To cook and please some rural family.
She overcame the cant and skew of slopes,
Some densely forested, some cleared for crops;
She often plucked and ate some nameless greens
Or sampled unfamiliar seeds and fruits,
Finding them sometimes sweet or savory
But caring only to appease desire,
For now the wildwood baby in her womb
    Commenced
   To make his unborn thirst
   And hungers felt, incensed
   Against existence, cursed
   With dooms his spirit sensed.

37.

To mortals, time in Wildwood's mystical,
The minuet of moments, hours, and years,
A dance no mortal being understands—
The man who wanders there for seven years
May find his house has sunk to nothingness,
His family all tucked into their graves,
Or else that only seven dawns have passed.
As Seren scaled the mountain range by day
And heights of sleep in Cavan's cloak by night,
She thickened, and the baby dozed or lurched,
His fairy-story growth ferocious, fierce,
Outlandish and preposterous in speed,
A burgeoning so rash and unrestrained
It seemed satanic, manic, half insane…
Like some grandfather's pocket watch wound tight
But then forgotten, Seren moved slower
And slower, mounting upward dreamily,
Her fingers finding comfort in the silk
Of rabbit fur, not daring to caress
The belly rippling with the characters
Of discord, battle, and hostilities,
          Letters
      That spelled out mutiny
      Against a womb's fetters;
      She shunned all scrutiny
      Of what was weird, yet hers.

38.

Atop the highest mountain, Seren met
What seemed a leafy garden walled by stones
That showed some marvelous ability,
Adjoining slabs fused tightly into one—
All day she paced the high plateau in quest
Of entrance, yet she found no passageways,
Nor any sign of threshold, gap, or gate.
But graceful branches trailed across the walls
To lend their fragrance to the mountain air,
And when a cobalt evening came, she camped
Underneath the scented canopy,
And as she dozed in Cavan's rabbit skins,
The cyclops moon stared freely at the girl
And peeped into the garden's mysteries.
The sounds of voices seeped into her drowse,
And singing lulled her deeper into sleep
As she let go the fear that she was lost
And now, perhaps, always to be adrift;
Then comforted, she rolled onto her side
And dreamed of Cavan fishing from a rock
While her two brothers splashed in rivulets.
        Pleasure
    Flooded into her dreams,
    Wonder without measure:
    The sight of boys in streams
    More than any treasure.

39.

The next day's hunt revealed no mystery,
And masonry remained inscrutable,
A stubborn riddle lacking any hint
That might have helped her breach its secrecy;
Again she slept and this time dreamed of home,
Hoeing weeds with her parents in the fields.
On the third day she walked until the stars
And moon appeared, and seemed so near and bright
They might be fruits among the canopy;
The light of stars and moon disclosed a gate,
Forged metal rippling like a watercourse
In a wash of starlight merged with moonbeams.
The gate was locked, but she could spy a swath
Of garden greensward, trees, and maypop vines
Blossoming around the stems of roses,
And farther back, a bowl of unhewn quartz
Shed water music, flinging drops in air,
And in a bower, Seren glimpsed a shape
That glimmered like a star inside a well,
    Half-seen
  And half unseen through bars,
  Some moonlit lady, queen
  Of blossoms, night, and stars,
  The axis of the scene.

40.

At dawn, on waking, Seren found the gate
And image of the garden quite dissolved,
The stone refusing to admit her hand,
All tint and starlight flown to memory,
The only region where a gleam remained…
She lazed a while in luxury of furs,
To conjure roses, lawn, and glimmerings.
"You sky-high door," she whispered, "why are you
Not meant for me, and where should I flit next?"
The garden made no audible reply,
Though Seren wished that she could catch the speech
Of leaves that murmured riddles overhead
And might unveil the where-and-how to go
Or why the lady's gate was sealed to her.
Resolving she would risk another path,
Seren searched the mountaintop and noticed
A downward trail, precipitous and straight
And shadowy, hemmed in by slanting firs
That made the way ahead mysterious.
"Yet was the lady my Greenmother goal
And guide to mend the woodland's loneliness?"
          Dry-eyed
     Though grieved to be alone,
     She put her fears aside
     And quit the walls of stone
     Where succor was denied.

41.

She still was anxious, stumbling down the path,
And wondered whether she was meant to stay,
To show persistence at the garden walls;
Told herself to trust her intuition
Of being disallowed and not let in—
That she might hunker down a hundred years,
Yet grasp no more than she already knew.
And more, the baby thumped inside her womb
As if he wished to breach placental walls
And leap to wilderness, his quickness strange,
Near supernatural, her belly's bulk
Beyond the count of ordinary days,
Though she had long lost track of numbering
The fleeing weeks and months, as in a dream.
The air grew dim and darkened suddenly
As trees pressed close, and ruts grew rockier
Until she had to steady each new step
By trusting to the help of mossy boles,
Feeling for branches that criss-crossed the way,
Afraid the firs conspired to halt her there
And cage her bones forever in the gloom.
        "Oh, trees!
     When will shade be over?
     Please end in sun, with bees
     Mining beds of clover
     And everything at ease."

42.

She felt no magic premonition's tap,
And yet the forest thinned and sunny fields
Appeared, a tillage feathery with plants
That proved to be small reddish-purple roots,
And never had she been so glad to taste
The earth and carrots or to see a pause
To trees that once had cast romance on her.
That night, while sleeping in the rabbit skins,
She dreamed of climbing upward to the gate
That forbade her steps, and slipping in, she
Found herself adrift beside a border
Of poppies, lilies, and forget-me-nots,
A glowing, cloudy mass of leaves and blooms
Wide open to the fertile light of stars.
Seren was changed, so slim and light a wand
She felt impelled to fly across the lawn,
As full of eagerness as any child
Who knows that life is an enchanted tale,
The very place for gaiety and play,
Although she stopped abruptly when she saw
The lady of the garden turn to look—
        And woke
    To find herself below
    The branches of an oak;
    Cauled around her torso
    Was Cavan's rabbit cloak.

43.

Some berries at the ragged edge of crops
Made Seren's morning meal before she tasked
Herself to compass the perimeter
Of rows and roots, to learn the length of fields
Snared between the steepnesses of mountains
And watered by the icy streams that sang
A merry tune while tumbling over rocks.
Rill and rindle, rivulet and runnel:
To see those waters sparkle in the sun,
All the ground seemed jocund, jaunty, gladsome,
And Seren felt her spirits buoyed high,
The youth in her resilient, soon renewed
By sleep and dreams, and by a sprig of hope
That the wildwood could still be a refuge.
To spy a cottage at the forest's edge
Could be a scary thing, the den of witch,
Conjuror, or prickly elvish creature,
But Seren, when she saw the luminous
Square of white at the margin of the trees,
Hesitated but a moment, searching
For signs of the anomalous and odd,
           And found
    No cause to be wary—
    No uncanny mound
    Of barrow wight or fairy,
    No cursed and blighted ground.

44.

A linen apron lashed around her waist,
Her hair in braids up-coiled into a crown,
The woman at the door looked welcoming
And greeted Seren like someone who knew
Her many years before and was made glad
To see her face again, grown older now
But showing features of a treasured child.
Though Seren questioned her, she only said
That she was here to help, and was no fay
Or demon, though she might be out of place,
As with many of the creatures roaming
Across the wildwood wilderness, where gates
To other times and other regions serve
As passageways for beings, good or ill.
"You needed me," she said, and gave a shrug;
"I sensed you wanted me, and so I came,
And here I am. It's just a simple thing."
But Seren felt they spoke two languages
And while she caught the woman's guileless words,
Their import slipped away from her and hid
In further questions, nebulous replies.
        "My name?
You may call me Wren—
Or Seult—it's all the same—
Or call me Emelynne,
Celestria, Yvaine."

45.

"You're not so sure of teasing, I suppose,
And therefore use my childhood's moniker,
And that was Wren, though later on I chose
Another tag, though not the ones I named:
How little any of us can discern
The lives beyond our own, but yes, I was
A tiny, tuneful fledgling known as Wren.
It seems so very long ago but now
I'll let the word fly back to me and nest,
And be the way you know to cry my name
Or think of me when we are kneading bread
Or stitching you a pair of proper shoes,
Or drawing out the threads from chaos-clouds
Of wool, its storms impaled on distaff sticks.
You see? I'll teach you how to weave a chant
Of praise to sing beside the fire at home,
For you will soon—you might not call it soon—
Find home again and carry all you learned
From dreams and swirling visions, from the dread
And beauty of the wildwood, zone of tests,
With windows onto Faëry, hell, and bliss.
    Your child?
  An uneasy matter,
  The sires not reconciled
  To deity: they scatter
  Discord, their hearts defiled."

46.

Thus Wren and Seren lived beside the field
And worked the weedy rows or planted seed,
Shaped a rustic tatterdemalion
Of rubbish, sticks, and flapping leaves that romped
In frolic winds or fluttered back and forth,
And wove a wattled fence around the house
To keep the looked-for child from wandering.
The chariot of sun made brilliant arcs
Across the sky so many times it seemed
That Seren might forget about her home,
So accustomed was she to the rhythm
Of days with Wren, so pleased to gather skills
That came like second nature to her friend,
And yet an hour of change was imminent.
Nights, she often dreamed of the Greenmother,
As she called the lady of the garden,
And paced a flower tunnel hung with snow,
Imbibing wisdom in her company,
Although the lady never spoke a word,
As if a beam of her mild starlight strength
Could be imparted by companionship.
     Despite
    The waywardness of time
    In wildwood lands, the night
    And day made peaceful rhyme,
    Sunlight twinned with dreamlight.

47.

As when abandoned souls were seized by flood
And drowning in a burst of cataracts,
Her waters broke, primeval deluge swept
From Seren, and chaotic cries upsurged:
A distant twang and booming deep inside
Her belly heralded the coming birth,
Unstoppable and fierce in its descent.
And she could hardly hear the voice of Wren
That called and called to her, and barely could
She feel the hand that grasped her own with strength,
For Seren was discarded, jettisoned
From sense and cast away in swirls of pain
Abolishing her self, her essence lost
In torrents of the infant's energies.
She felt her body split in agony,
The monstrous baby ramming at her doors,
Relentless force that cared no whit for her
But flung its passionate and ireful life
Against the incandescence of her flesh
That blazed and sang in reckless holocaust
As kindled sap, ascending, sings of fire.
     The child
  Careened into the air;
  Already roiled and riled
  And sensing arms as snare,
  He boiled with spleen and bile.

48.

Wren cauled the giant boy in swaddling cloth
And left him free to howl, so she could tend
To Seren, fainted from the press of pain;
With every particle of energy
He bucked and kicked and wrestled mightily,
Protesting life in every inch of flesh,
Proclaiming fury, spirit, passion-fire.
But dreaming Seren drifted on the grass
And curled to rest at the Greenmother's feet;
The lady plucked an apple from a tree
To slowly pare it with a silver knife,
And then she let the golden peel go free,
Its shining body slithering through stems,
While Seren ate the pieces one by one.
To her it seemed she lived inside the walls
For days, and for the first time heard a tune
The lady sang, and saw the stars respond
And dance as though delighted by the pour
Of wordless notes, the pulse of mystery
That was the living current of a flood
That washed the garden with fertility.
                Never
       Did Seren ask to leave,
       Nor did she endeavor
       To wake, but wished to cleave
       To the dream forever.

49.

When Seren swam up from her long repose,
She woke to struggle, shrieks, and anarchy:
The baby strove against his swaddling bands,
Loudly clamoring for food and freedom,
Growling, groaning, ululating, barking
Syllables and hellish vocables
Suggestive of the sound of sentences.
And though she tried to nurse him with her breasts,
The newborn had surprising strength to bite
And bruise the fragile skin with nubs of teeth
Already broken through his infant gums,
As seemed incredible, unnatural,
And freakish, though it did not seem to strike
Surprise from Wren, who only shook her head.
"He is exactly what he is," she said,
"Hermetic progeny of god-king, god,
And mortal flesh, as happened long ago
Around the world in profane rituals—
Still can happen when a fallen angel
Conspires with human weaknesses to sire
A being two-thirds god, one-third human,
    At least
  In Wildwood where a lamb
  Like you is tupped and fleeced
  Of honor: a temple scam
  Once common, not yet ceased."

50.

In weeks and months to come, the baby raged
Against restraint, and crawling to the field
Began to grub and gobble purplish roots
Till his skin became like rosy carrots,
And nothing the two women tried could make
Him bear their coaxings or obey their words,
This infant prince: imperious and proud.
The whirling wheel of months gave way to years,
And often Seren felt a mother's life
Meant suffering and inability
To change the spread of cards her fate had dealt,
Maternal martyrdom so wildwood-weird,
She hardly could recall the days before
She heard the sugared words of Ariel.
And rarely did she dream the garden gate,
For sometimes just the walls of stone appeared,
Or else a massive lock secured the bars,
And she could only look and long to be
In the garden with the starlit lady,
Meandering on paths through clouds of bloom,
Underneath the dancing stars and moon.
    But Wren
  Was always true to her,
  An ever-constant friend,
  Companion through the blur
  Of years: gift and godsend.

51.

This boy of rosy carotene increased,
His queerly-colored skin was matched by hair
And eyes of the same shade, and even teeth
Though if the tint was native, natural,
Or from the strictly carrots-only fare
Was not entirely clear in Seren's mind,
As he was hard to read in every way.
Tempest-tossed, he grew more rude with years,
A monstrous toddler given to mad fits
That made the women shove him out-of-doors
Until the thunderstorms of temper waned;
A barbarous boy who yanked his mother's hair
And liked to kick her shins to black-and-blue,
Who stamped on all her tenderness of heart.
"I've absolutely failed," she said to Wren,
"At teaching him of love and courtesy,
And sometimes feel I'd like to be a child
Once more and dream of what one day I'd be,
Inventor, storyteller, herbalist,
A mother of a flock of little lambs,
A finer daughter than I was before.
        Undone
    By my savage giant,
    Unfettered, feral son
    Who'll never be pliant
    Or care for anyone."

52.

He learned to gormandize on yellow squash,
To snatch and gorge on pickle-worms and moths,
To pounce on rabbits, mice, and whistle-pigs,
Or any helpless, burrowing small snip
Of furry vigor… *Pompon Maximus,*
Wren dubbed him, *Curcurbita Maxima,*
And seldom did she style him by his name.
His mother called him for her father, half
Remembered and with kinder sentiment
Than she had felt when living in his house,
Though *Wilkin* seemed too fair a tag for one
So wholly passionate and uncontrolled,
And often she would brand him *Hawk* or *Wolf*
When he snuffed and hunted in the hedges.
"Little Demon won't stay longer with us,"
Wren prophesied, though "little" was no apt
Term for one who shot up six feet tall
When he was less than seven years of age;
And Seren wept, as much for her defeat
As for the coming loss of Wilkin, son
Who wrung her heart with purgatory woe:
        "I prize
    The love that might have been,
    And all my deepest sighs
    Are for the lying-in
    That led to shocked surprise."

53.

Yet Seren didn't give up on her boy,
Reciting tales that once her parents told
When seated cosily beside the hearth:
The stories of good-hearted fools who thrived
By kindness and a clever cat or horse
That bonded with the simple innocent
And flung him through adventure's grinding mill.
She recounted Psyche luring Eros
But losing by the lifting of a flame
To contemplate exactly what she'd won—
So Psyche hunted hill-and-vale for love,
Demanding news from witches, clambering
The peaks of sleep, the depths of wakefulness,
And wearing out three pairs of iron shoes.
She sang the tales that rose in her like dreams,
With filmy, evanescent figurines
That slowly moved through hurt and tragedy,
Ascending to elysiums of joy…
And for a moment burned on mountaintops
In pouring light and revelation's fire,
Glimpsing what the journey meant for them.
    Wilkin
   Hated Seren's stories,
   Whether rough or silken,
   Loathed a vision's glories,
   Poor twisted devilkin.

54.

Although he often uttered grunts and groans,
Her Wilkin spoke as well as a grown man:
"My ghostly fathers, who and what are they,
For I hear murmurs in my head that twine
Like snakes or move like your long braided hair
That winds together in the fingers' flash
But also is three parts and endless threads.
Sometimes a tongue will tell me father-names,
Say he is Mephistopheles or Toad;
Sometimes it claims that he's another one,
Behemoth, Andromalius, Man-sphinx,
And muddles me with wormy trickery,
Makes me hate the squash-vine-borer voices
That mock with words or by not answering.
He summons me to jump, and I won't do
His bidding, no! yet still I do the thing
That spirals in my skull like melon-worms,
To bite some silly mouse or vole that squeaks
And shakes off every bit of squirming life,
Or bellow till I cannot hear the song
Of Wren who soothes the father-beast in me.
        I want
    And yet I don't know what…
    The snaky voices haunt
    My mind like dirty smut
    On leaves; they tease and taunt."

55.

Then Seren said, "I heard one voice that spoke
In feigning accents, beautiful and sweet,
Yet I repent of listening to him,
And though I didn't understand the tones
Meant only domination, evil's rule,
I chose to listen and became a friend
And confidant to what I couldn't see.
Under the streaming floods of wildwood years,
I bend, I yield, I do forgive the words
And hurtful acts that marred me in the past,
For I was also twisted and confused
By living close to death, by childhood grief,
Though now I'm full of sympathy for those
Once near and known—you gave that gift to me."
But Wilkin hardly listened, understood
So little what his mother said to him
Because the words that slithered in his head
Were coils that caught his thoughts: complexity,
A wildwood snake that curls around a branch
And seems to master every compass point
In winding, being in them all at once.
     The bob
   And wheel of passing days
   Only increased the throb
   Of voices, built the maze
   That trapped a noisy mob.

56.

The torments that he felt, that Seren wished
To calm and comfort were too great to heal,
For there were times when Wilkin viewed himself
As ill-shaped monster and abortive lump,
Rosy-carotene abomination,
And then he hurled wolf-howlings at the moon
Or lobbed rock-bombs and clods against the sun.
On the bad days when Seren clutched her head
And sobbed as if her heart and mind must crack,
The yawn of chaos sought to swallow her,
Though Wren was there to take her by the hand
And render mother-sympathy to one
Who bore her motherhood uneasily,
Who sometimes floated in despair's abyss.
Wren spoke of light and vision, clarity
Of purpose, promised Seren would find home
And dream again of open garden gates,
Go wandering in clouds of flowerbeds,
Content and singing words to beautify
Her world and heal the misbegotten past,
Although her prophecies seemed fantasy:
   Fancy;
  A wish chimerical;
  Lineless chiromancy;
  A spinning, spherical
  Run at gyromancy.

57.

One morning Wilkin chased the mice and hares,
Raced to overthrow the green-man scarecrow,
And stomped the field of carrots, stuffing roots
Into his mouth as if he might devour
The tidy rows, the hand-tilled earth, the world:
Crunching hard, the rosy pieces spilling
With tremendous tears that soaked his tunic.
Seren went to soothe her giant fledgling,
Grown larger than a man yet still a child,
Round-cheeked, big-eyed, strange-tinted, hair a shock,
His limbs made sturdily, this chubby boy
Afflicted by the wildwood's mysteries…
And Seren tilted up her face to peer
Into his eyes, so alien and bright.
He stopped his tears and made a grab at her,
Close-clasped and clenched her as she called his name—
Then fled, his mother tucked beneath one arm,
His legs pounding, jolting on bumpy ground
As Seren glimpsed the sky, the dirt, and Wren
In clipped succession—trees then closing in
While he raced faster, faster, far from home;
          Bereft
     Of choice and power, she
     Gasped for voice and breath;
     Unable to break free,
     She feared impending death.

58.

Was it for seven days or seven hours
She was hauled by Wilkin through the wildwood?
What did the visionary voices say,
And how did angels shrill like burning stars?
Or was she lurching through a land of pain,
Gone mad with hunger, thirst, and misery,
Hallucinating lights and starry song?
He hurled her into dark from a low cliff
And staggered on, while she sailed out and down,
The wind caressing her as if a hand
Intended help and touched with gentleness,
Her mother's necklace flying, lost in gloom—
Her body crashed into a thorny tree
That held her like an offering to skies.
Her skin was blossoming with many mouths
That sang back to the stars, and she was pierced
And open to the starlight and their song,
And whether she was flowing in or out,
Or what it was that poured in cataracts
As if she must be filled, must be emptied,
She couldn't tell, for flesh was merged and blent
   With star
  And tree and flood of song
  That fell to her from far—
  From space, from stellar throng,
  From night's deep reservoir.

59.

The world was rack, the world was blood-stained thorns,
The world was body tumbled to the tree…
And Seren heard a pulse like tinnitus
That seemed the proof of Wilkin's crashing flight
With footsteps moving ever off from her,
Until a silence said that he had gone
And stolen all her motherhood away.
She floated in the bonfire of her pain,
And how it might instruct she did not know,
Except that longing, anguish, and relief
Can wind like serpents in the wilderness
To make one rippling braid—as long ago,
Plaiting her mother's hair, she came to learn
That bitterness and grief may twine with love.
Seren, Seren, Seren… A thread of breeze
That wove a way between the spiny boughs
Seemed whispering its sibilance to her
In accents that perhaps belonged to Wren
Or else the Lady of the Mountaintop
And conjured glimmerings of memory,
Confused and fragmentary images.
        She wept.
     Her brambled agony
     Went on. She woke or slept
     Commingled with the tree,
     Catastrophe's adept.

60.

She dreamed that time unreeled back to the start:
She saw the universe was sung and made,
As she herself was sung and made again
While thorns and wounds and star-fire sang her name
And figures holding golden bowls passed by,
Mist rising from the basins like white flame,
And faces looked out from the radiance.
Later, when she called those hours back,
She wondered if she saw her brothers there,
Their faces shining silver through the mist,
Remembered how the thorns were tipped with blood
And glittered like a glory in the dawn,
How every little leaf and twiglet gleamed
And trembled with its freight of messages.
Entranced, she moved among the golden bowls
And knew herself to be akin to them,
Her body jarred around a mounting mist:
"Inside my heart's a mountaintop," she cried,
"Where figures drift and starlight gardens steam
With balm that censers canopy and sky;
I break apart, embracing paradise…
    The whole
  Of me cradles mountain
  And stars; I am a bowl
  Of spume, body's fountain
  Of mind and heart and soul."

61.

At last, she climbed to earth and crept away,
The thorn tree stark against the morning sky,
The memory of revelation blurred
To softness in her mind… to her surprise,
She found Wilken had tossed her at the edge
Of Wildwood, and she recognized the spot
As not so far from family and home.
After, when she took her parents' hands
And visited the brothers' graves, she learned
They thought that she had only been away
For moments, and that all her seven years
In Wildwood was a magic tale to them,
And giant Wilkin but a fantasy,
No near relation to their settled lives.
She often thought of him, the lady, Wren,
The mountaintop, and how in secrecy
She might become a golden bowl of flame
In an enchanted world—this one, a place
Of paradise and hell and mundane hours,
Where she could learn to make, to sing her tale
And be a mistress of the marvelous
    Around
  A hearth and wildwood blaze
  On nights in winter crowned
  By the strange, striking lays
  That hold mortals spellbound.

ABOUT THE AUTHOR

MARLY YOUMANS lives at the brink of James Fenimore Cooper's Glimmerglass, in a small, often-snowy village with two stone castles, a blurring of the line between local fact and Cooper fiction, a surfeit of ghosts, an Indian mound, and a seldom seen glacial lake monster. She makes poems, stories, and novels, especially when it snows, and sometimes they win awards—the Michael Shaara, the Ferrol Sams, a Silver ForeWord BOTYA, and others. Marly's books include: a recent novel, *Charis in the World of Wonders*; a recent collection of poems; *The Book of the Red King*; and a prior book-length poem, *Thaliad*. *Seren of the Wildwood* is her sixteenth book.

ABOUT THE ILLUSTRATOR

CLIVE HICKS-JENKINS is a Welsh artist/illustrator with a particular collaborative attachment to poets. He has illustrated several books for the current British Poet Laureate Simon Armitage, including Faber & Faber editions of *Sir Gawain and the Green Knight* and *The Owl and the Nightingale*. Clive and Marly have been working together for fifteen years, during which time he has produced artworks for all but one of her book covers. Before embarking on *Seren of the Wildwood* he illustrated the forthcoming Seamus Heaney translation of *Beowulf* for Folio Society.

www.ingramcontent.com/pod-product-compliance
Lightning Source LLC
Chambersburg PA
CBHW041326110526
44592CB00021B/2839